Contents

GRAMMAR SECTION TESTS

SECTION 1: Nouns

SECTION 2: Pronouns — 5

SECTION 3: Adjectives — 9

SECTION 4: Verbs — 13

SECTION 5: Adverbs — 17

SECTION 6: Sentences — 19

SECTION 7: Conjunctions, Interjections, Punctuation, and Capitalization — 23

SECTION 8: Diagramming — 27

GRAMMAR SUMMATIVE TESTS

SECTIONS 1–2: Nouns & Pronouns — 31

SECTIONS 3–4: Adjectives & Verbs — 33

SECTIONS 5–6: Adverbs & Sentences — 35

SECTIONS 7–8: Conjunctions, Interjections, Punctuation, and Capitalization & Diagramming — 37

WRITING TESTS

CHAPTER 1:
Writing Skills — 39
Writing Prompt — 41

CHAPTER 2:
Writing Skills — 43
Writing Prompt — 45

CHAPTER 3:
Writing Skills — 47
Writing Prompt — 49

CHAPTER 4:
Writing Skills — 51
Writing Prompt — 53

CHAPTER 5:
Writing Skills — 55
Writing Prompt — 57

CHAPTER 6:
Writing Skills — 59
Writing Prompt — 61

CHAPTER 7:
Writing Skills — 63
Writing Prompt — 65

CHAPTER 8:
Writing Skills — 67
Writing Prompt — 69

SECTION 1 TEST Nouns

Underline the singular nouns once and the plural nouns twice.

1. Several passengers offered a seat to an elderly woman.
2. Five watches in this display case are quite expensive.
3. The plumber used a set of wrenches to remove the rusty bolts.
4. Some sheep were grazing in the field behind the barn.
5. My parents investigated the sequence of loud noises in the garage.

Write the plural form of each noun.

6. match _____
7. woman _____
8. half _____
9. moose _____
10. battery _____
11. portfolio _____
12. potato _____
13. leaf _____
14. sister-in-law _____
15. prey _____

Circle each misspelled plural noun.

16. Many students carry heavy backpacks to their classeses.
17. Did you place the clean dishs and plates on the shelfs?
18. A few motoristes stopped to watch the deers grazing in the meadow.
19. Mosquito are often a problem around the patioes at sundown.
20. I ordered my beef tacoes with green oniones but no tomatoes.

Write *concrete* or *abstract* to identify each noun.

21. pencil _____
22. wisdom _____
23. patience _____
24. artifact _____
25. restriction _____
26. murals _____

Underline the concrete nouns and circle the abstract nouns.

27. Those firefighters showed true bravery during the fire last night.
28. The joy on their faces brought tears to my eyes.
29. Determination will help you find success in your future.
30. The protestors are requesting equal rights for all workers.

Circle whether each underlined noun is a subject (*S*) or a subject complement (*SC*).

31. <u>Brianna</u> was the winner of the debate.   S   SC
32. Phuong is the <u>president</u> of the biology club.   S   SC
33. Few <u>people</u> have traveled this far into the desert.   S   SC
34. These copper <u>pots</u> are relics of an ancient civilization.   S   SC
35. The poem that Shauna wrote is a lovely <u>tribute</u> to her mother.   S   SC

Underline the simple subject and circle the subject complement in each sentence.

36. Beth's new pet is a brown and white puppy.
37. Her ancestors were early pioneers in Kansas.
38. The city of New York is a favorite tourist destination.
39. My parents are volunteers at a local senior activity center.
40. The families along this street are all sports enthusiasts.
41. An example of a literary genre is poetry.
42. This song that my brother composed is an excellent melody.

Underline the nouns used as direct objects and circle the nouns used as indirect objects.

43. His grandmother sent Ken a postcard.
44. Anthony gave me his jacket.
45. She and her brother bought Maggie a set of colored pencils.
46. The babysitter read the child a very funny story about penguins.
47. Coach Mendez gave the team directions for the final play.
48. The travel agency offered each student a discount ticket for a ride on the train.
49. As a gesture of good faith, the company offered customers a refund.

Underline each noun used as an object of a preposition.

50. Jackson and I both read books about astronomy.
51. We scoured the beach for aluminum cans and glass bottles.
52. Sea stars of many varieties clung to the tidepool rocks.
53. The population of sea otters was the greatest number in a decade.
54. All cushions on the sofa were soiled by the dog's feet.
55. The crowd of protestors remained behind the fence at the end of the alley.

SECTION 1 TEST Nouns (continued)

Circle whether each underlined word is a direct object (*DO*), an indirect object (*IO*), or an object of a preposition (*OP*).

56. A red rose is a symbol of true <u>love</u>.   DO IO OP
57. I donated <u>money</u> to several charities this year.   DO IO OP
58. The newest museum exhibit features <u>masks</u> from Mexico.   DO IO OP
59. Eileen bought her <u>sister</u> several framed pictures for her room.   DO IO OP
60. Toss <u>Wendy</u> the softball this time.   DO IO OP

Write the possessive form of each noun.

61. friend _____
62. paths _____
63. Chris _____
64. men _____
65. investigators _____
66. witness _____

Underline each possessive noun and circle the thing owned or possessed.

67. Have you read Gary Paulsen's latest book?
68. We found Josh's keys under Julius's jacket.
69. The women's hats worn to the Kentucky Derby's festivities are quite elaborate.
70. Even the detectives' determination couldn't help them find the case's solution.

Underline each possessive noun. Circle whether each sentence shows separate possession (*S*) or joint possession (*J*).

71. Tina's and Tim's homes are both near the park.   S J
72. We applauded after Ari and Sheila's lively duet.   S J
73. I browsed through Jack's and Pete's comic books.   S J
74. Carla's and Bruce's stories about camp are hilarious.   S J
75. Luis and Russ's presentation was very informative.   S J

Underline the appositive and circle the noun it explains.

76. Our new puppy, a Chihuahua, chews on my shoes.
77. My sister Joan is a classical pianist.
78. John Grisham, a writer of popular legal thrillers, is my favorite author.
79. Josh's sister Elia collects *manga*, Japanese comic books.

Underline the appositive or appositive phrase. Circle whether it is restrictive (R) or nonrestrictive (N).

80. Her friend Simon is a doctor. R N
81. Paris, the City of Light, is my favorite place. R N
82. Our guests, visitors from Norway, want to see the Grand Canyon. R N
83. The presenter, an expert on medieval life, enthralled the audience. R N
84. The word *sonrisa* means "smile" in Spanish. R N
85. This architectural landmark was once home to the composer Tchaikovsky. R N

Write *noun* or *verb* to identify each underlined word.

86. The smell of rotten garbage was awful. _____
87. Snakes prey on smaller animals. _____
88. The day of the race is tomorrow. _____
89. We can shop for vintage clothes at the swap meet. _____
90. Draw a quick sketch before you begin painting. _____

Write *noun* or *adjective* to identify each underlined word.

91. The rock walls had crumbled. _____
92. Pioneers used the river to transport people and cargo. _____
93. I always wear my rain boots on wet spring days. _____
94. The top of the mountain was enveloped in clouds. _____
95. The space program trains people to become astronauts. _____

Read the following paragraph. Then respond to the questions.

> Our town has a community garden. This land used to be a vacant lot. Now people grow fruits, vegetables, and flowers here. My family's plot includes tomatoes and carrots. My brother Joel planted sunflower seeds. I planted sweet corn.

96. What is the subject of the first sentence? _____
97. Rewrite the misspelled plural noun correctly. _____
98. What is the appositive in the fifth sentence? _____
99. Underline the possessive noun.
100. In the fourth sentence, circle the nouns used as direct objects.

SECTION 2 TEST   Pronouns

Underline each pronoun. Write *first*, *second*, or *third* to identify the person of each underlined pronoun.

1. Did she help Henry?
2. Ashley brought me muffins for breakfast.
3. They thanked the chef for the delicious meal.
4. Mrs. Barrett warned us not to be late for class again.
5. You can hang that jacket in the closet.
6. She is teaching me how to crochet this scarf.

Underline each singular pronoun once and each plural pronoun twice.

7. They told me where to find the computer store.
8. She will be attending the lifeguard program with us.
9. Can we take Renee and him to the library before it closes?
10. Chris, can you wrap these packages and deliver them for me?
11. I don't know where he put the keys, but I will help you find them, Ron.
12. Arnold and I have found the lost dog, and we returned it to her.

Underline each pronoun. Write *male*, *female*, or *neuter* to identify the gender of the pronoun.

13. Lisa was late, and she missed the speech.
14. This kitten is adorable, but it sheds too much fur.
15. Mrs. Nichols reminded her to take home the books.
16. Trevor and he handed the cashier the money.
17. Can Kelly or Sara take it to the cafeteria?

Circle the antecedent of each underlined pronoun.

18. David was thirsty after <u>he</u> jogged so far.
19. The car stopped because <u>it</u> ran out of gas.
20. Sandra thinks that <u>she</u> left her purse at the restaurant.
21. We can frame these photographs or put <u>them</u> in an album.
22. My aunt and I raked leaves, and <u>we</u> stuffed them into garbage bags.
23. Ann and Beth folded the clean clothes and put <u>them</u> in the dresser.

Underline each intensive pronoun and circle each reflexive pronoun.

24. Hailey will buy herself a new dress for the event.
25. The students themselves chose the theme for the yearbook.
26. I myself have submitted several poems for publication.
27. A daily journal might help you learn more about yourself.

Underline each pronoun. Circle whether the pronoun is a subject (*S*) or a subject complement (*SC*).

28. We play card games in the evening.   S   SC
29. The owners of the home are they.   S   SC
30. The player with the most rebounds in the game was I.   S   SC
31. Each afternoon he gives piano lessons in his home.   S   SC
32. Have you ever tried gazpacho, a cold soup?   S   SC

Circle the pronoun or pronouns that correctly complete each sentence.

33. (Us   We) sat by the open window.
34. The best speaker in the debate was (she   her).
35. After much consideration, the final winner was (he   him).
36. The ones that caused the commotion earlier were Noelle and (they   them).
37. (He   Him) and (me   I) will probably finish our project before the weekend.

Underline each object pronoun. Circle whether it is a direct object (*DO*), an indirect object (*IO*), or an object of a preposition (*OP*).

38. Jessica sent him a card.   DO   IO   OP
39. These skateboards belong to Justin and me.   DO   IO   OP
40. Friends will offer you support in times of need.   DO   IO   OP
41. Elsa and Gwen may meet us later at the mall.   DO   IO   OP
42. If they are muddy, please leave them outside the door.   DO   IO   OP

Circle the pronoun or pronouns that correctly complete each sentence.

43. (I   me) may ask Tony to join us for lunch.
44. The cashier handed their purchases to (they   them).
45. Her grandmother is showing (she   her) how to hem her jeans.
46. Glen bought a scooter and plans to ride (it   them) to work.
47. On Saturday mornings Mom and (him   he) make pancakes for Sam and (we   us).

SECTION 2 TEST Pronouns (continued)

Underline each possessive pronoun and circle each possessive adjective.

48. The locker on the top is yours.

49. Do you know if these gift-wrapped packages are ours?

50. Her use of metaphors is not as impressive as mine.

51. His friends have not seen your new bike yet.

52. Our house is fine, but theirs was damaged by its rising floodwaters.

Write a contraction for each pair of words.

53. he is _____
54. it is _____
55. I will _____
56. she will _____
57. they have _____
58. we have _____
59. they are _____
60. it shall _____

Use the instructions in parentheses to write a demonstrative pronoun that could replace each noun.

61. pen (far) _____
62. ax (near) _____
63. lids (far) _____
64. fox (far) _____
65. baskets (far) _____
66. orange (near) _____
67. girls (near) _____
68. crowd (far) _____

Circle each demonstrative pronoun. Write whether it refers to something *near* or *far*.

69. Whose shoes are these? _____

70. As you can see, this is my brother's backpack. _____

71. Is that the couch you bought at the yard sale? _____

72. Those belonged to my aunt, and they aren't for sale. _____

73. These are the items that are in the best condition. _____

Circle each interrogative pronoun. Write whether it refers to a *person* or a *thing*.

74. What is the capital of Ohio? _____

75. With whom did you attend the concert last Saturday? _____

76. Which of these CDs did you enjoy the most? _____

77. Who invented the lightbulb, and how long did it take? _____

Underline each indefinite pronoun.

78. Anyone can attend the concert.
79. Has everyone submitted a permission slip for the field trip?
80. We can't do anything about the changes in the weather.
81. This spicy salsa is enjoyed by only a few.
82. Neither will admit to leaving something behind on the bus.
83. Jill has nothing to say about the decisions that affect so many made by some.

Circle whether each underlined pronoun is singular (*S*) or plural (*P*).

84. Both ordered soup and salad for lunch.   S P
85. Would someone please close the window?   S P
86. Much has been written and debated about Shakespeare's plays.   S P
87. Does anyone know how to get to the courthouse?   S P
88. I can't believe that nobody said anything about the surprise party.   S P
89. On this list of hotels, several offer lower rates in winter.   S P

Circle the indefinite pronoun or pronouns that complete each sentence.

90. There was not (nothing   anything) I could do.
91. (No one   Anyone) wants to leave early and miss the final encore.
92. Sadly, Gerald realized he had (anything   nothing) to eat for dinner.
93. Doesn't (no one   anyone) have a flashlight I can borrow for a moment?
94. We had plenty to drink, but (no one   anyone) brought any cups.
95. Didn't (anyone   no one) buy napkins or (anything   nothing) else to clean up spills?

Read the following paragraph. Then respond to the questions.

>Carolina's father is a gourmet chef. He taught hisself how to cook everything from herb-roasted chicken to stuffed salmon. On Friday nights Carolina's father cooks dinner for us. His is the most delicious spaghetti I have ever tasted.

96. What is the antecedent of *He* in the second sentence? _____
97. What is the pronoun in the third sentence? _____
98. Is this word a subject pronoun or an object pronoun? _____
99. Underline the incorrect reflexive pronoun. Rewrite it correctly. _____
100. Circle the possessive pronoun.

Name _____ Date _____

SECTION 3 TEST Adjectives

Underline each descriptive adjective and circle the noun it describes.

1. Our new home has an unkempt backyard.
2. I just met that friendly fellow in the pointy hat.
3. The bear rubs against the rough bark of the tree.
4. Which brave person will ride that enormous roller coaster next?
5. Canada geese, majestic and grand, often migrate to warm climates in winter.

Underline each definite article. Circle each indefinite article.

6. Ashley drank an iced coffee with her muffin.
7. Where did you put the toothpaste?
8. We gave the filthy dog a bath after lunch.
9. Brian is watching a movie in the living room.
10. An index is a list of all the topics in a book.

Write the correct indefinite article before each noun.

11. _____ calculator
12. _____ igloo
13. _____ bookmark
14. _____ bridge
15. _____ hummingbird
16. _____ honor

Underline each numerical adjective and circle the noun it describes.

17. Jake spent three hours on his homework.
18. My bedroom is on the second floor.
19. The first tour leaves in eight minutes.
20. Our second baseman made the third out.
21. After reading 35 pages of the fourth chapter, I fell asleep in five seconds.

Circle the numerical adjectives that correctly complete the sentences.

22. This exam will last (four   fourth) hours.
23. His soccer team finished (three   third) in the league.
24. The (two   second) book in the series is better than the (one   first) book.
25. After preparing my chili for (five   fifth) days, I won (two   second) prize in the cook-off.
26. (One   First) month is approximately (30   30th) days or (four   fourth) weeks long.

Underline each subject complement and circle the noun it describes.

27. These pretzels taste very salty.
28. That skyscraper on the corner is huge.
29. Some singers felt nervous before the audition.
30. For some reason my sister seems sad today.
31. Several members of the youth orchestra are quite talented.
32. The novel's main character, Ramona, is hilarious and mischievous.

Write the comparative and superlative forms for each adjective.

33. long _____ _____
34. slow _____ _____
35. happy _____ _____
36. silly _____ _____
37. good _____ _____
38. graceful _____ _____
39. sullen _____ _____

Underline each descriptive adjective and write whether it is *positive*, *comparative*, or *superlative*.

40. Kate is the tallest member of the team. _____
41. I am a faster runner than any of my friends. _____
42. My biggest fear is giving a speech in front of the class. _____
43. Who is a better dancer, Taj or Miguel? _____
44. This cave is darker than I remember it. _____
45. Jen's performance received complimentary reviews. _____

Circle the correct adjectives that complete the sentences.

46. This box is (heavier   heaviest) than that one.
47. Who is the (younger   youngest) member of the class?
48. Alex seems (more   most) careful than his brother.
49. These students were the (noisier   noisiest) ones on the bus.
50. I am a far (better   best) tennis player than a softball player.
51. Your cough sounds (worse   worst) today than it did yesterday.
52. I'm (more   most) generous these days, but Abe is the (less   least) selfish person I know.

SECTION 3 TEST Adjectives (continued)

Use *little* or *few* to write a phrase that describes each noun.

53. money _____

54. recipes _____

55. time _____

56. water _____

57. customers _____

58. solace _____

Write *less* or *fewer* as needed to complete the sentences.

59. Mel's room has _____ space than mine.

60. Donna took _____ classes last quarter.

61. Our new house has _____ bedrooms than the previous one.

62. Dora spent _____ money on her vacation than Julie did.

63. Why are there _____ oranges on the tree this year?

64. I have _____ wealth than many, but I also have _____ problems.

Circle the adjectives that correctly complete the sentences.

65. This club has the (least   fewest) members.

66. Which highway has the (least   fewest) traffic?

67. This mattress provides the (least   fewest) amount of support.

68. For this upcoming year, the (least   fewest) students signed up for the cooking class.

69. The candidate with the least experience received the (least   fewest) votes in the election.

70. One trunk held the (least   fewest) coins, but another had the (least   fewest) weight.

Use the directions in parentheses to write demonstrative adjectives to complete the sentences.

71. _____ invitations look quite elegant. (near)

72. What is making _____ strange sound? (far)

73. _____ battered journal belongs to my older sister. (near)

74. _____ students are new members of the Ecology Club. (far)

75. I am pleased with the way _____ mosaic turned out. (near)

76. We haven't tried _____ café, but I do like _____ one. (far, near)

Underline each interrogative adjective and circle the noun it modifies.

77. Which team won the contest?
78. Do you know whose backpack this is?
79. What accessories do they sell here?
80. Whose locker is the one below yours?
81. Which figurine did Carly buy, and whose gift will it be?

Underline each indefinite adjective and circle the noun it modifies.

82. Many residents attended the meeting.
83. No student is a harder worker than Katrina.
84. This particular mountain peak has been scaled by few climbers.
85. Neither musician has more experience than Rudy.
86. I think both applicants will do well in either position.
87. Some police officers spoke to several witnesses about the accident.

Underline each adjective phrase and circle the noun it describes.

88. We enjoyed the sandwiches from the deli.
89. The capital of Egypt is Cairo.
90. Did you receive an invitation to the graduation ceremony?
91. The dazzling jewels in that necklace are blue diamonds.
92. All the photographs on this wall are portraits of celebrities.
93. The clown in the baggy red pants is the silliest one in the show.

Read the following paragraph. Then respond to the questions.

> Our city's new aquarium is quite impressive. It is the third largest in the state. Visitors can observe and learn about everything including tiny sea horses, exotic jellyfish, and playful otters. The most large crowds gather around the shark tank. Many people want to see these deadly predators up close.

94. What is the subject complement in the first sentence? _____
95. Underline the numerical adjective. Does it express number or order? _____
96. What is the indefinite adjective? _____
97. Write the superlative adjective correctly. _____
98. Circle the descriptive adjectives in the third sentence.

Name _____   Date _____

SECTION 4 TEST Verbs

Underline each verb or verb phrase. Write whether the verb form is *present*, *past*, *past participle*, or *present participle*.

1. We walked through the garden after lunch. _____
2. My dog buries its toys in the backyard. _____
3. Colorful hot-air balloons are floating over the valley. _____
4. The Warners offered a reward for the return of their cat. _____
5. Many scholars have researched the history of the painting. _____

Write the past form for each verb.

6. call _____
7. cry _____
8. give _____
9. break _____

Write the past participle form for each verb.

10. wish _____
11. stop _____
12. speak _____
13. write _____

Circle the verb that correctly completes each sentence.

14. Please (sit   set) the lamp on this table.
15. The sun is (rising   raising) over the mountain.
16. That sleepy cat has been (laying   lying) on the bed all day.
17. Do you know who (let   left) all these dirty dishes in the sink?
18. Katherine can't recall where she (lay   laid) her purse and car keys.

Circle the transitive verbs. Underline the doers once and the receivers twice.

19. Lorena makes her own clothes.
20. We planted pink tulips under the kitchen window.
21. An Australian kangaroo carries its young in a pouch.
22. Mr. Wilson, the emcee, commanded our attention and introduced the performers.

Underline the intransitive verb or verb phrase in each sentence.

23. The excited students waited impatiently.
24. This author often writes about his disobedient dog.
25. A chilly winter wind is blowing from the west and is freezing the plants.

Underline each verb or verb phrase. Write whether it is *transitive* or *intransitive*.

26. The small rubber ball rolled under the bed. _____
27. Today's robots are performing many new functions. _____
28. At one time most U.S. immigrants arrived at Ellis Island. _____
29. Tania placed those reference books on the top shelf. _____
30. Tim is currently growing a variety of fruits in his orchard. _____

Underline each linking verb and circle each subject complement.

31. These photographs look very old.
32. This shiny blue fabric feels so smooth.
33. The elderly man and woman at the door are my grandparents.
34. After many years of training, Linda became a surgeon.
35. The new salesclerk felt apprehensive about asking her boss for a raise.

Write the simple past tense for each verb.

36. watch _____
37. paint _____
38. make _____
39. say _____
40. tell _____
41. sink _____
42. become _____
43. be _____

Underline each verb or verb phrase and write its tense.

44. I make my bed every morning. _____
45. Dania quickly ran to first base. _____
46. A total lunar eclipse will occur tonight. _____
47. The fishers hoist the heavy nets onto the deck. _____
48. My sister and I are going to try sushi for the first time. _____

Complete each sentence with the verb in parentheses in the progressive tense indicated.

49. I _____ a Spanish class this year. (take—present)
50. We _____ the concert. (attend—future)
51. The lawyers _____ simultaneously to the judge. (speak—past)
52. Scientists _____ the effects of pollution. (study—present)
53. Each group _____ their reports. (present—future)
54. Six people _____ for this position at the bank. (apply—past)

Name _____ Date _____

SECTION 4 TEST Verbs (continued)

Underline each perfect tense verb phrase. Write whether it is in the *present perfect* or *past perfect* tense.

55. Sean has visited the science center many times. _____

56. The judges have evaluated each artist's entry. _____

57. Kristen had learned French before her trip to Paris. _____

58. Prior to the audition, they had rehearsed their parts often. _____

Underline each singular subject once and each plural subject twice. Circle each verb or verb phrase.

59. Darcy brought potato salad for the picnic.

60. Tiny hummingbirds are hovering above the red flowers.

61. This innovative display features information about "going green" in the home.

62. Cornell, Shannon, and I are planting sunflower seeds in the garden.

Circle the verb that correctly completes each sentence.

63. An architect (designs   design) many types of buildings.

64. There (is   are) several ways to explore the Grand Canyon.

65. Pete (doesn't   don't) know if the cat is hiding somewhere upstairs.

66. (Was   Were) you able to find a book about Roman gladiators?

67. The articles in this magazine often (focuses   focus) on healthy cooking tips.

Write whether each sentence is in the *active* or *passive* voice.

68. Helen hung clean towels in the bathroom. _____

69. The parade was attended by thousands of people. _____

70. The Nguyens welcomed the Stones to the neighborhood. _____

71. Several photographs were taken by that photographer. _____

Underline each verb in the indicative mood.

72. This survey was conducted by a research group.

73. Stacy has written a lengthy report on the Civil War.

74. Who are the four presidents on Mount Rushmore?

75. The scholarship committee is still accepting applications for the upcoming year.

Underline each verb phrase in the emphatic mood.

76. We did learn much about Sweden on our trip.
77. Dan and Jan do support their daughter's music career.
78. A hawk does hunt other smaller birds while in flight.
79. Several witnesses did indeed see the suspect leave the scene of the crime.

Underline the verb in each sentence. Write *yes* or *no* to identify whether the verb is in the imperative mood.

80. List your sources at the end of your report. _____
81. An aqueduct transports water from one place to another. _____
82. Plant these flower bulbs six inches below the soil's surface. _____
83. How did they create this elaborate ice sculpture? _____

Circle the verb in the subjunctive mood that correctly completes each sentence.

84. I wish my homework (was   were) finished.
85. Julie wishes it (was   were) not too late to meet her friends.
86. If I (was   were) you, I'd review all my notes before this test.
87. The council requested that we (be   were) at the meeting on time.

Underline each modal auxiliary once and each main verb twice.

88. Mai can play three different musical instruments.
89. My sister Giselle might design the logo for Dad's business cards.
90. He must drive his younger sister to her piano lessons.
91. Marty may haul this garbage to the dump, but he should certainly do it soon.

Read the following paragraph. Then respond to the questions.

> Rome started as a group of villages. It becomed the center of a great empire. In the Colosseum spectators watched gladiators fight. The Forum was the center of political and commercial life. Rome's streets were lined with shops and temples. New structures were added by many Roman emperors. Rome's ruins can still be seen today.

92. What tense is the verb in the first sentence? _____
93. Is the verb *watched* transitive or intransitive? _____
94. Underline the incorrect past tense verb. Write it correctly. _____
95. What is the linking verb in the fourth sentence? _____
96. Circle the verb in the passive voice in the sixth sentence.

SECTION 5 TEST Adverbs

Underline each adverb. Write whether it is an adverb of *time*, *place*, or *manner*.

1. I often jog through the park. _____
2. We stopped here for lunch. _____
3. Shane always makes his bed in the morning. _____
4. The shy girl walked nervously to the podium. _____
5. I immediately felt the warm sun when I walked outside. _____

Write an adverb of manner for each adjective.

6. slow _____
7. bright _____
8. careless _____
9. hopeful _____
10. thoughtful _____
11. severe _____

Underline each adverb. Write whether it is an adverb of *degree*, *affirmation*, or *negation*.

12. The children are very happy. _____
13. We have never eaten at this restaurant. _____
14. I hardly recognized Jane after her new haircut. _____
15. Mr. Harding allegedly sold his house for a million dollars. _____
16. I had not reviewed my class notes before the biology test. _____

Write the comparative and superlative form of each adverb.

17. late _____ _____
18. early _____ _____
19. quickly _____ _____
20. peacefully _____ _____
21. well _____ _____

Circle each comparative or superlative adverb. Underline the verb or verb phrase the adverb describes.

22. Helen studies more than her friends.
23. Ian is hitting the ball harder than the other ballplayers.
24. Of all the customers, Mr. Kwon was waiting most patiently.
25. I signed up more willingly for cleanup duty than my friends did.

Write *adjective* or *adverb* to identify each underlined word.

26. Rebecca performed <u>poorly</u> during her audition. _____

27. These blueberry muffins look <u>delicious</u>. _____

28. A cat's tongue actually feels quite <u>rough</u>. _____

29. The man seemed <u>calm</u> after the accident. _____

30. All the students spoke <u>well</u> during the debate. _____

Circle the word or phrase that correctly completes each sentence.

31. (No   Any) other person cooks as well as Rashelle.

32. We haven't (never   ever) been to Florida before.

33. There (was   wasn't) hardly enough water available for the runners.

34. Nobody (attended   didn't attend) the early morning meeting yesterday.

35. Jordan (hasn't   has) but one game token left in his pocket.

36. The fans in the back of the stadium (could   couldn't) barely see the stage.

37. Hillary and her sister are (ever   scarcely ever) late for their classes.

Underline each adverb phrase once and each adverb clause twice.

38. I drink hot tea when I have a cold.

39. Mr. Watkins helped us learn about our town's history.

40. The doctor's next patient is waiting in the examination room.

41. You must marinate the chicken before I can grill it on the barbecue.

42. Unless the weather clears, we will have to move the party inside.

43. Because Sasha missed the bus this morning, she rode in the neighbor's carpool.

Read the following paragraph. Then respond to the questions.

My sister and I are often competitive. Maya runs fast than I do, but she has never beaten me in a game of basketball. I play the piano quite well. Maya hasn't never learned an instrument because she prefers to sing. Consequently, I play the music while she sings along.

44. What is the adverb of time in the first sentence? _____

45. Circle the error in the second sentence. Write it correctly. _____

46. Is the word *well* used as an adjective or an adverb? _____

47. Underline the double negative and write it correctly. _____

48. Underline twice the adjective clause in the last sentence.

Name _____ Date _____

SECTION 6 TEST Sentences

Underline each complete subject. Circle each simple subject.

1. All firefighters must wear protective gear.
2. Some plants produce colorful flowers.
3. The elderly man stopped to rest for a moment.
4. These Aztec temples look similar to the pyramids in Egypt.
5. Each member of the team must attend daily practice.
6. Any one of these reasons should be enough to get people to act.

Underline each complete predicate. Circle each simple predicate.

7. Hank works as a computer technician.
8. Several small birds are hiding under this bush.
9. Blood carries food and oxygen throughout the body.
10. Many snow-capped peaks tower above the small mountain village.
11. Thousands of people will visit the historic site this year.
12. All the buyers of the product must agree to the terms of the contract.

Draw a line between the subject and the predicate. Circle the simple subject and underline the simple predicate.

13. Antarctica is the region around the South Pole.
14. My sister can use these leaves for her collage.
15. These old photographs document our town's early history.
16. Most of the crowd did not understand the tour guide's directions.
17. Last summer my brother Bill and I voluntarily served as ranch hands in Wyoming.
18. A set of books, all first editions, remain in the locked cabinet.

Write whether each sentence is in *natural* or *inverted* order.

19. The new community park has two soccer fields. _____
20. How are frogs and toads alike? _____
21. The novel's resolution came as a shocking twist. _____
22. Above the flowers hovered a tiny hummingbird. _____
23. On the other side of these trees is a small lake. _____

Section 6 • 19

Write whether each sentence is declarative (D) or interrogative (I). Then add the correct end punctuation.

24. How tall is the Hoover Dam
25. These tour buses can each hold 50 passengers
26. Why were you unable to complete the assignment on time
27. Which of these two poems did you like better
28. A handheld compass will help you navigate back to the campsite

Write whether each sentence is imperative (I) or exclamatory (E). Then add the correct end punctuation.

29. Wow, I can't believe we are in India
30. Stop that silly behavior immediately
31. Hey, that's an amazingly lifelike portrait
32. Please return your reply card in the enclosed envelope
33. What a magnificent sight the Eiffel Tower is

Write whether each sentence is *simple* or *compound*.

34. James read a book, and I watched a movie.
35. Tennis and volleyball are my favorite athletic activities.
36. A penguin's feathers keep it warm in the freezing cold.
37. Juan and Ana can go sailing, or they can sit on the beach.
38. Pat wanted to stay and relax, but she had to return to work.

Add the correct punctuation to each compound sentence.

39. We walked to the corner café but it was closed.
40. These appetizers are delicious they just melt in your mouth.
41. The concert was sold out yet some fans were able to obtain tickets.
42. Strong waves rocked the boats and gusty winds unfurled their sails.
43. The Smithsonian is amazing it includes many museums and several research centers.

Underline each prepositional phrase. Circle each preposition.

44. The clothing store opens at noon.
45. My cousin Kyle is sitting between his parents.
46. I hung my coat in the hall closet when I got home.
47. Stan and Mark are walking rapidly toward the parking lot.
48. The squirrel found several nuts on the ground and hid them under the big sycamore.

SECTION 6 TEST Sentences (continued)

Circle the preposition that correctly completes each sentence.

49. The lifeguard dove (in   into) the pool.
50. These visitors are staying (at   to) a luxury hotel by the beach.
51. The campers decided to walk (at   to) the lake.
52. Our class must choose (between   among) Ryan and Serena for president.
53. I just can't decide (among   between) red, blue, or green for the car's color.
54. (Beside   Besides) Jessica, did anyone else forget money for the entrance fee?
55. In this photograph the foreign exchange student is standing (beside   besides) us.

Write whether each underlined word is used as an adverb (A) or a preposition (P).

56. A bee is buzzing near my ear. _____
57. A crowd of people wandered past. _____
58. The enormous passenger plane landed on the runway. _____
59. We can review your answers after the test. _____
60. Temperatures this spring are far below normal. _____
61. When we arrive at the museum, we will look around first. _____

Underline each adjective phrase. Circle the word the phrase describes.

62. The gift for Emily is a diamond necklace.
63. This stew utilizes vegetables from my garden.
64. Elaine sent me a postcard of the Taj Mahal.
65. Several students in this class are studying Latin.
66. This party of four people requested a large table near the window.
67. The unusual markings on this tablet are examples of ancient writing.

Underline each adverb phrase. Circle the verb the phrase describes.

68. The autumn leaves are falling to the ground.
69. Steam slowly rises over the china cup.
70. Several people suddenly gathered around the fountain.
71. For six months I volunteered at the animal shelter.
72. Overcome by curiosity the boy peeked into the large brown box.

Underline each prepositional phrase. Then write whether the phrase is an adjective phrase (*ADJ*) or an adverb phrase (*ADV*).

73. Summer is my favorite time of year. _____
74. Our only soccer ball is rolling down the hill. _____
75. These flowers are a gift for my mother. _____
76. An unusual noise was coming from those bushes. _____
77. Friends from his neighborhood visited John in the hospital. _____
78. A large group of people is waiting outside the building. _____

Underline the adverb clause in each sentence.

79. My dogs bark whenever I use the vacuum cleaner.
80. While Alma listened to music, I did a crossword puzzle.
81. We missed our flight because we could not find a cab.
82. Jonah will wait here by the curb until the next bus arrives.
83. Corina may go to the game provided that her chores are finished.
84. Unless Jeff saves more money, he cannot afford to go on the cruise.

Write whether each underlined clause is independent (*I*) or dependent (*D*).

85. They saw a variety of animals when they visited the zoo. _____
86. Robby is cranky today because he did not get enough sleep. _____
87. After the presentation the speaker will answer your questions. _____
88. Since I won the raffle, I will take you to lunch after the party. _____
89. Jason takes his dog with him wherever he happens to go. _____
90. While the patient waits, the dentist will prepare the replacement tooth. _____

Read the following paragraph. Then respond to the questions.

> Did you know that a penguin is a flightless bird? Its feathers keep it warm and its wings propel it through the water. A penguin's diet consists mainly of fish. Look at its bill. The hook at the end helps a penguin hold onto its slippery, wriggly food.

91. Circle the imperative sentence.
92. What is the adverb phrase in the second sentence? _____
93. Is the third sentence simple or compound? _____
94. What is the complete subject of the third sentence? _____
95. Underline the compound sentence. Add the correct punctuation.

SECTION 7 TEST: Conjunctions, Interjections, Punctuation, and Capitalization

Underline the conjunction in each sentence.

1. These repairs are costly but essential.
2. We bought fresh fruits and vegetables at the farmer's market.
3. The movers packed the boxes and loaded them in the van.
4. Erik sprinted toward the finish line yet lost the race.
5. Today's meeting with the council was neither productive nor informative.
6. We can take a harbor cruise or ride bikes along the marina.

Circle each conjunction and underline the words it connects. Write whether it connects *nouns*, *verbs*, *adjectives*, or *adverbs*.

7. Did you know some plants capture and eat insects? _____
8. They saw a sea star and a sea urchin in the tide pool. _____
9. The cat moved noiselessly and stealthily toward its prey. _____
10. One day Stuart will be a well-known musician or composer. _____
11. This novel's main character is quiet and mysterious. _____

Write whether each conjunction connects prepositional phrases (*PP*) or independent clauses (*IC*).

12. We can camp near the river or between these trees. _____
13. Arthur will lead the meeting, or he may take the minutes. _____
14. They wanted to watch the movie, but it was sold out. _____
15. Candidates for this program must possess skills in math and in science. _____
16. Kisha handled the awkward situation with grace and with humor. _____
17. After he had finished, Matt placed the papers in a folder and on a shelf. _____

Underline each interjection and add the correct punctuation.

18. Aha I knew I'd find you here.
19. Ugh That bag of garbage needs to go in the trash.
20. Ouch My ankle is still sore from when I tripped and fell yesterday.
21. Whew I wasn't sure I'd be able to walk up four flights of stairs with this box.
22. My word I never knew what a talented writer you were.

Circle the interjection that correctly completes each sentence.

23. (Ouch   Well)! I think I just stepped on a nail.
24. (Alas   Bravo)! Your performance was amazing.
25. (Yikes   Ha)! We just narrowly missed hitting that large rock in the road.
26. (What   Beware)! There is a large dog roaming around outside.
27. (Whew   Sh)! I've been working for hours, but I finally completed my essay.

Add periods to each item where needed.

28. P T Barnum
29. 4 ft by 3 in
30. 2900 Oak Ave
31. Pets R Us, Inc
32. Monday, Sept 17
33. Dr M B Bashir

Add periods to these sentences where needed.

34. His title is Gen Glen Williams He is retired
35. Please mail this package You must get to the post office by 5:00 p m
36. Use 1 pt of vinegar and 2 gal of water to make this cleaning solution
37. Mr and Mrs Kim's address is 100 W Ridgemoor Blvd, Boise, ID
38. Author R L Stine is signing books here at 9:00 a m on Sat, Aug 15

Add commas to these sentences where needed.

39. The wedding will be held on June 4 2011.
40. Nashville Tennessee is the location of the family reunion.
41. Joanne can drive to the mall or she can take the bus.
42. We bought a new couch two chairs and a table for the living room.
43. Mrs. Cole my art teacher is a talented sculptor and painter.
44. This summer camp in Frankfort Michigan offers swimming canoeing and archery.
45. Hal told the clerk "I wrote my birthdate March 23 1985 at the top of the form."

Add the correct end punctuation to each sentence.

46. Wow! That was a close call
47. What an amazing sight this is
48. Did Isaac bring the popcorn for our movie night
49. Paragliding, a combination of sailing and surfing, is a popular sport
50. Were you able to find someone who can fix the leak in the roof

SECTION 7 TEST Conjunctions, Interjections, Punctuation, and Capitalization
(continued)

Add semicolons to these sentences where needed.

51. I'm going home I'm too sick to stay at school.
52. Nina is a fierce competitor she never gives up.
53. The Grand Canyon is a popular tourist site its natural grandeur is amazing.
54. We have visited Cairo, Egypt Tokyo, Japan and Mumbai, India.
55. Terryl has lived in Memphis, Tennessee Orlando, Florida and Newport, Oregon.

Add a colon to each item where needed.

56. Dear Mrs. Wallace
57. Pack these items thick socks, hiking boots, and a canteen.
58. So far we've studied these habitats the forest, the desert, and the tundra.
59. Dear Governor Williams
60. These are my areas of interest horticulture, ornithology, and ecology.

Add quotation marks and commas to these sentences where needed.

61. Benjamin Franklin said A penny saved is a penny earned.
62. We are reading a short story, The Monkey's Paw by W. W. Jacobs.
63. Edgar Allan Poe's poem The Raven is one of my favorites.
64. The Long Road Home is a magazine article about Iraqi war veterans.
65. Do you know who said We have nothing to fear but fear itself ?

Write *yes* or *no* to identify whether each sentence is correctly punctuated.

66. My book report is on *The Call of the Wild.* _____
67. I'm rehearsing a scene from Shakespeare's play "The Tempest." _____
68. Mark Twain said, "If you have nothing to say, say nothing." _____
69. *60 Minutes* is a popular television news series. _____
70. Judith knows the words to the song "Over the Rainbow." _____
71. I would like to know who said, "Imagination is more important than knowledge?" _____

Section 7 • 25

Add an apostrophe to each item where needed.

72. Angela's journal
73. class of '11
74. Let's go.
75. Write two t's.
76. the summer of '09
77. She'll find its collar.

Rewrite each word, adding hyphens to show how it can be broken into syllables.

78. concern _____
79. sincere _____
80. beautiful _____
81. gymnastics _____
82. reliable _____
83. formulaic _____

Rewrite each compound word, adding hyphens where needed.

84. fiftyfive _____
85. onesided _____
86. selfportrait _____
87. editorinchief _____
88. merrygoround _____
89. twoyearold _____

Use the proofreading mark (≡) to identify which letters should be capitalized.

90. last summer i worked as a lifeguard.
91. her ancestors migrated here from the east.
92. mrs. choi said, "have you met my brother, phil?"
93. my cousins live in grand rapids, michigan.
94. this book is about president john f. kennedy.
95. the play is titled *a raisin in the sun*.

Read the following paragraph. Then respond to the questions.

George Washington Carver was a prolific inventor. Born a slave around July 12 1864 Carver went on to become famous in several ways: scientist botanist and educator. He is credited with discovering over 300 uses for peanuts. Carver said "Ninetynine percent of the failures come from people who have the habit of making excuses."

96. What is the punctuation mark in the first sentence? _____
97. Punctuate the date in the second sentence correctly.
98. Circle where a punctuation mark is missing in the last sentence.
99. Add commas where are they are needed to separate items in a series.
100. Which compound word should be spelled with a hyphen? _____

SECTION 8 TEST Diagramming

Circle the simple subjects and underline the simple predicates. Diagram the sentences.

1. The shy girl is smiling nervously.

2. These African parrots are squawking noisily.

Circle the direct objects and underline the indirect object. Diagram the sentences.

3. The happy bride tossed the beautiful bouquet.

4. My parents gave me a gold bracelet.

Circle the subject complement. Diagram the sentence.

5. These fresh strawberries taste sweet.

Section 8 • 27

Circle the appositives in the diagrams. Then circle the letter of the sentence that matches each diagram.

6.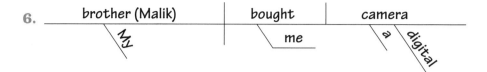

   a. My brother Malik bought me a digital camera.

   b. Malik, my brother, bought me a digital camera.

7.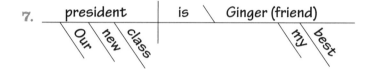

   a. Our new class president is my best friend Ginger.

   b. Our new class president is Ginger, my best friend.

Circle the intensive pronoun and underline the reflexive pronoun. Diagram the sentences.

8. I knitted the baby's sweater myself.

9. Ethan made himself a turkey sandwich.

SECTION 8 TEST Diagramming (continued)

Circle the prepositional phrase in the diagram. Then circle the letter of the sentence that matches the diagram.

10. Nora | is reading | books
             \about
               \exploration
                  \space

   a. Nora is reading books about space exploration.

   b. Nora is reading a book about space exploration.

Circle the compound sentence part in each sentence. Diagram the sentences.

11. Marcus and Aiden play on the same basketball team.

12. Wendy reviewed and revised the final draft of her essay.

Circle the conjunction in the sentence. Diagram the sentence.

13. Gary wants a lizard, but I want a hamster.

Circle the interjection in the sentence. Diagram the sentence.

14. Oh no! I spilled coffee on my white shirt.

Circle the conjunction in each diagram. Then circle the letter of the sentence that matches the diagram.

15.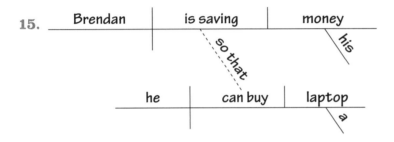

   a. Brendan is saving his money so that he can buy a laptop.

   b. Brendan is saving his money so he can buy a laptop.

16.

   a. I listened to music as I was making dinner.

   b. As I was making dinner, I listened to music.

Diagram the sentence.

17. We quickly cleaned the mess in the kitchen before our parents returned from the store.

Name _____ Date _____

SUMMATIVE ASSESSMENT

SECTIONS 1–2 Nouns & Pronouns

Underline singular nouns once and plural nouns twice. Circle those that are both.

1. atlas   deer   basements   alarm   Chinese

Underline each subject. Circle each subject complement.

2. The owner of the spa is Helen.
3. English is my favorite subject.

Write whether each underlined noun is a *direct object*, an *indirect object*, or an *object of a preposition*.

4. Docents can provide information about a museum's exhibits. _____
5. Blowfish is another name for a pufferfish. _____
6. The police officer issued the driver a warning. _____

Underline the appositive phrase. Write whether it is *restrictive* or *nonrestrictive*.

7. Baklavah, a sweet pastry, is my favorite dessert. _____
8. The singer Isaiah Stone is promoting his latest album. _____

Insert apostrophes to show correct ownership.

9. the mens restrooom
10. Wayne and Nicoles baby sister
11. her mother-in-laws birthday
12. Lewiss and Kims lockers

Underline the subject pronouns and circle the object pronouns.

13. You and I can meet them at the marina at noon.
14. They gave her a ride to the airport.
15. Karen and he have already mailed the letters to you and me.

Underline the possessive pronouns and circle the possessive adjectives.

16. Ours is parked next to their blue van.
17. Her shoes and his boots were more expensive than mine.

Underline each indefinite pronoun. Circle whether it is singular (*S*) or plural (*P*).

18. Either would make a good topic for a report.   S P
19. These art materials should be given to both.   S P
20. No one wants to help me wash the dog.   S P

Read the passage. Then proofread it, using proofreading marks to make corrections. Look for 10 mistakes related to nouns and pronouns.

A medieval castle was home to many peoples. Each castle had a great hall where it's residents ate and slept. The lord of the castle was very wealthy and powerful. In addition to the castle itself, he owned all the surrounding land. Knights and squires also lived here. Squires knights in training spent seven years learning how to defend the castle before they were made knights himselves. Numerous servants, including a steward, several cookes, and many pages, were also part of life in the castle. This people oversaw the entire estate, cooked the food, cleaned the chambers, and cared for the horses. The lords peasants farmed his land, but they did not live in the castle. Their was a hard life. As much as these peasants worked, they could not do nothing to improve their situation.

Name_____ Date_____

SUMMATIVE ASSESSMENT

SECTIONS 3–4 Adjectives & Verbs

Circle each adjective and underline each verb.

1. solve   predict   honorable   slender   intelligent   threw

Write whether each underlined adjective is *demonstrative*, *interrogative*, or *indefinite*.

2. I had several opportunities to retake the history test. _____
3. Where did you find that antique lamp? _____
4. Whose explanation did you find more convincing? _____
5. No one understands the situation as well as those people. _____

Underline each adjective phrase and circle the noun it describes.

6. The artifacts in this display are believed to be 2,000 years old.
7. The author of that novel is a native of South Africa.

Write whether the underlined verb phrase is *transitive* or *intransitive*.

8. That cruise ship will depart promptly at noon. _____
9. Marta has been reading at the library for an hour. _____
10. We are collecting canned goods for the food bank. _____

Underline each subject once and each subject complement twice. Circle each linking verb.

11. These colorful fish are extremely expensive.
12. My friend Rose remains calm no matter what happens.
13. Lawrence seems weary after his long drive.

Write whether each sentence is in the *active* or *passive* voice.

14. Many seeds were stored next to the tree by those squirrels. _____
15. The championship game was watched by a nervous crowd. _____

Write whether each sentence is in the *imperative*, *emphatic*, or *subjunctive* mood.

16. Create a list of reasons that support your argument. _____
17. I wish I were able to attend the concert with you. _____
18. Chris did return the lost dog to its owner. _____

Read the passage. Then proofread it, using proofreading marks to make corrections. Look for 10 mistakes related to adjectives and verbs.

On September 12, 1940, fourth teenagers made an incredible discovery near Lascaux, France. The boys accidentally stumbled upon a cave and will discover prehistoric cave paintings that depicted an variety of animals. Researchers has estimated that these paintings are between 16,000 and 17,000 years old.

The caves became a popular tourist site. However, over time, the human presence in the cave caused changes in temperature and humidity. This changes began to damage the paintings, and the caves were closed to the public in 1963. Scientists and preservationists have worked hard since that time to restore and preserve the artwork priceless.

Today, only a little people have access to the cave. Scientific experts is allowed brief visits, while others work hard to combat a fungus that threatens the paintings. Visitors must still get some sense of the original artwork at Lascaux II, an alternative site that replicates some of the cave's famousest images.

Name _____   Date _____

SUMMATIVE ASSESSMENT

SECTIONS 5–6 Adverbs & Sentences

Match each word to the correct type of adverb.

1. positively _____   a. adverb of degree
2. very _____   b. adverb of manner
3. finally _____   c. adverb of affirmation
4. not _____   d. adverb of place
5. skillfully _____   e. adverb of time
6. here _____   f. adverb of negation

Circle each adverb. Underline each adjective.

7. Warren feels bad because he performed poorly on the test.
8. Ms. Rios is happy that the children play so well together.

Underline each adverb phrase once and each adverb clause twice.

9. The two opposing teams are running onto the football field.
10. The ring with the ruby belongs to my grandmother.
11. Whenever I go to the beach, I build a sand castle by the water's edge.

Underline the simple subject and circle the simple predicate in each sentence.

12. The tiny caterpillar will become a stunning butterfly.
13. A large group of customers is waiting at the cash register.

Circle whether each sentence is simple (*S*) or compound (*C*).

14. Because of the long line, he will miss the beginning of the movie.   S C
15. Sherry wants to make an omelette, but she has no more eggs.   S C

Underline each prepositional phrase. Circle each preposition.

16. The puppies dashed across the yard and into the house.
17. Henry can sit between us or across the aisle.

Circle whether the underlined word is a preposition (*P*) or an adverb (*A*).

18. Did you see a gray cat walk <u>past</u>?   P A
19. We can spend some time looking <u>around</u> the shops downtown.   P A

Summative Assessment • 35

Read the passage. Then proofread it, using proofreading marks to make corrections. Look for eight mistakes related to adverbs and sentences.

On an average weekday, over two million commuters go in and out of Tokyo's Shibuya Station, passing by a large bronze statue of a dog, Hachiko. The statue was erected in 1934 to honor this dog's unwavering loyalty to its owner? Today Hachiko's statue is a popular meeting place in the train station.

Every morning Hachiko watched his master leave for work. Every evening the dog greeted his master at the train station. One day the man suffered a stroke and died at work. Hachiko still waited patient for his owner, who never returned.

Eventually, a new owner adopted Hachiko, but the dog would most frequently run away and return to the train station. People couldn't hardly believe their eyes each time this happened. Many commuters recognized Hachiko. They felt badly for the dog and brought him food and water. Hachiko maintained this daily routine for ten years. The story of this faithfully dog spread throughout Japan, and people eventual honored him with a statue. To this day, Hachiko remains a symbol of loyalty.

Name _____ Date _____

SUMMATIVE ASSESSMENT

SECTIONS 7–8 Conjunctions, Interjections, Punctuation, and Capitalization & Diagramming

Circle each conjunction. Underline each interjection.

1. Good! We have enough time to ride the subway or take a taxi.
2. Gosh! You have quite a collection of baseball cards and sports posters.
3. Whew! I dropped this bowl, but it didn't break.

Add the correct end punctuation to each sentence.

4. How were you able to solve the mystery so quickly
5. What an awesome vista this is

Add commas, semicolons, or colons to each sentence where needed.

6. Most flowers have these three parts a stamen a pistil and a sepal.
7. Nelson Amos was the town's first mayor this park is named for him.
8. Here is the time capsule it won't be opened until Sunday July 4 2077.

Add quotation marks to each sentence where needed.

9. I am reading Sun-sational Getaways in this travel magazine.
10. Anne Frank wrote, No has ever become poor by giving.

Circle each compound word that is correct.

11. fourth-floor   forty-four   first aid   up-to-date   selfmotivated

Circle the conjunction in the diagram and the letter of the matching sentence.

12.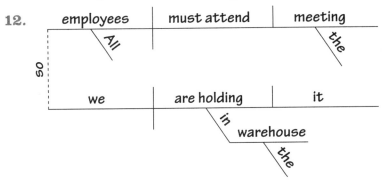

a. All employees must attend the meeting, so we are holding it in the warehouse.
b. All employees must attend the meeting; we are holding it in the warehouse.

Summative Assessment • 37

Read the passage. Then proofread it, using proofreading marks to make corrections. Look for 15 mistakes related to conjunctions, interjections, punctuation, and capitalization.

the White House has been home to over forty U.S. presidents. But did you know that it has also been the home to a wide variety of pets In recent years the presidents home in Washington, DC, has included assorted cats and dogs, but earlier presidents welcomed more unusual animals.

President Abraham Lincolns son had a pet turkey named Jack. Jack came to be Thanksgiving dinner to the White House, but Lincoln's son asked Lincoln to pardon the bird. This led to the White House tradition of pardoning a turkey each Thanksgiving.

During World War I, President Woodrow Wilson let his herd of sheep graze on the White House lawn. The sheep kept the grass cut: so no one needed to mow it.

In the 1960's White House pets continued with President John F Kennedy and his family. The Kennedys had all these pets a cat dogs birds hamsters and ponies. Their daughter's pony; Macaroni, pulled her on a sled across the White House grounds.

CHAPTER 1 TEST Writing Skills

Write the numbers 1–5 to place each set of words in alphabetical order.

1. ____ gauze   ____ guardian   ____ genial   ____ glimpse   ____ gallery
2. ____ freestyle   ____ flying   ____ freedom   ____ ferrous   ____ ferment

Write whether each word is found *before*, *on*, or *after* this dictionary page.

> technician   telephone

3. telecast _____   6. tempest _____
4. teach _____   7. technical _____
5. tedious _____   8. technology _____

Use the dictionary entry to answer the questions.

> **so • lo (sō´lō) n. A piece of music played or sung by one person.** *Danny stood on the stage alone for his solo.* **adj. Done by one person.** *This is a solo piece for the violin.* **v. To fly a plane alone.** *The young pilot soloed his first flight.*

9. What parts of speech are listed for *solo*? _____
10. How many syllables does *solo* have? _____
11. How many meanings does *solo* have as an adjective? _____
12. What part of speech is used in this sentence?
    Emma is ready to perform her solo. _____

Revise each rambling sentence by making shorter sentences and combining ideas.

13. Taking care of a puppy is a lot of work because you have to give it food and you have to give it water and take it for walks every day.

    _____

    _____

14. Our picnic at the park was a disaster because Casey forgot the food and Ed spilled juice on the blanket and then a swarm of bees descended on us.

    _____

    _____

Rewrite each run-on sentence correctly.

15. A sari is a brightly colored garment many women in India and Pakistan wear saris.
_____
_____

16. Snorkeling is my favorite activity I love to explore the world below the surface of the water.
_____
_____

Circle the word that has a more exact meaning.

17. I poured cold (liquid   lemonade) in each guest's glass.
18. Henry held up his hands as he (sprinted   ran) to the finish line.
19. Corinne offered to bring (clothing   items) for the yard sale on Saturday.
20. We are (happy   thrilled) with our new purchases.
21. I found this novel I just finished to be (awesome   spellbinding).

Write a more exact and vivid word for each overused word.

22. said _____
23. large _____
24. eat _____
25. car _____
26. unhappy _____
27. good _____

Complete the word web with more exact and vivid words for *brave*.

28.
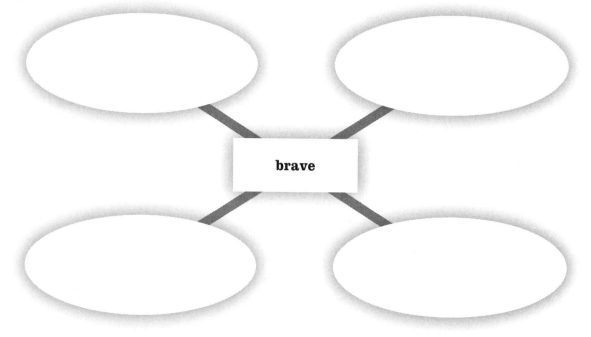

40 • Chapter 1

Name_____ Date_____

CHAPTER 1 PROMPT Personal Narrative

1. Read the prompt carefully.
2. Plan and organize your writing on this page.
3. Write your personal narrative on the back.
4. Revise and proofread your personal narrative.

PROMPT: Think of an outdoor experience that you have had. Write about your experience. Include interesting details that your classmates might like to read.

Plan your personal narrative here. Use a word web, a time line, or notes.

Chapter 1 • 41

Your personal narrative will be graded on how well it
- is planned.
- maintains a clear focus.
- is organized using chronological order.
- shows personality.
- uses words that are exact and natural.
- uses a variety of sentence types and lengths.
- is free of grammar, usage, spelling, and punctuation errors.

Write your personal narrative here. Refer to your plan as you write. Use another sheet of paper if needed.

Name _____ Date _____

CHAPTER 2 TEST Writing Skills

Underline the transition word or phrase in each sentence.

1. First, wash and dry each piece of fruit.
2. Prepare the cheese topping while the pasta is cooking.
3. Gather a variety of beads, and then sort them into cups by color.
4. The second step is folding the paper in half.
5. To finish, use a paint pen to sign your name.
6. Soak the seeds in cold water, and after that lay them flat to dry.

Use proofreading marks to add transition words and phrases.

7. Glue four craft sticks to create a square frame. Add self-stick foam shapes to decorate the frame. Use tape or glue to attach a photograph to the back of the frame.

Write *simple*, *compound*, or *complex* to identify each type of sentence. Underline any coordinating and subordinating conjunctions.

8. Rafael wants to read, but we want to see a movie. _____
9. This painting will look amazing in our living room. _____
10. You must clean your room as soon as you get home. _____
11. Before I go to the store, I need to make a shopping list. _____
12. His uncle talks about baseball all the time. _____
13. Tim can play backgammon with us, or he can play cards. _____

Rewrite each pair of simple sentences as a compound sentence. Circle each coordinating conjunction.

14. Kayla enjoys watching tennis. She plays soccer.
    _____

15. You can heat water on the stove. You can heat it in the microwave.
    _____

16. I practice my serve often. I still hit the ball into the net.
    _____

Chapter 2 • 43

Rewrite each simple sentence as a complex sentence by adding a clause and a conjunction.

17. We rushed to the driveway.
   _____

18. The head coach meets with the players.
   _____

19. The exhausted runner collapsed.
   _____

20. **Read the directions for operating a dishwasher. Fill in the flowchart, using the information from the directions.**

   1. Place dishes in dishwasher.
   2. Add soap. Choose desired setting. Push "Start" button.
   3. If dishwasher does not start, check that the door is closed.
   4. If dishwasher still doesn't operate, call technician.
   5. Let clean dishes cool before removing them.

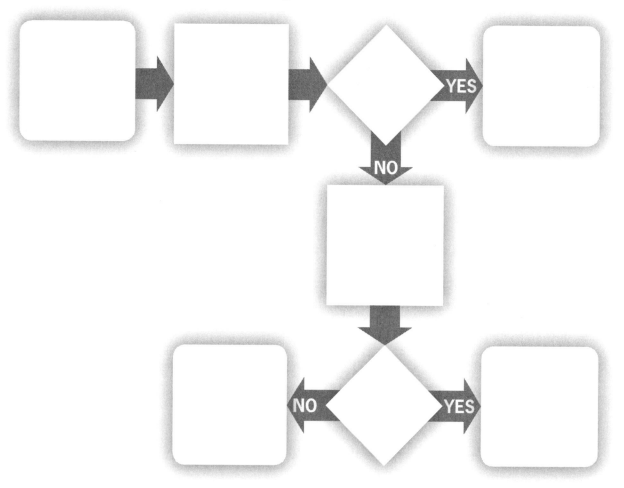

44 • Chapter 2

Name _____ Date _____

CHAPTER 2 PROMPT How-to Article

1. Read the prompt carefully.
2. Plan and organize your writing on this page.
3. Write your how-to article on the back.
4. Revise and proofread your how-to article.

PROMPT: You have a friend who has never used a thesaurus before. Write a how-to article explaining how to find a synonym for *large* in a thesaurus. Be sure to include clear step-by-step directions.

Plan your how-to article here. Use a flowchart, a numbered list, or notes.

Chapter 2 • 45

Your how-to article will be graded on how well it
- is planned.
- states a clear purpose.
- provides instructions that are detailed, accurate, and complete.
- presents the steps in logical order.
- uses appropriate tone and concise, imperative sentences.
- includes transition words and language specific to the topic.
- is free of grammar, usage, spelling, and punctuation errors.

Write your how-to article here. Refer to your plan as you write. Use another sheet of paper if needed.

Name _____ Date _____

CHAPTER 3 TEST Writing Skills

Write whether each sentence appeals to the sense of *sight*, *sound*, *smell*, *taste*, or *touch*.

1. The rough, dry bark of the dead tree scraped his arm. _____
2. Trey's mouth puckered up from the pickle's salty sourness. _____
3. The howling wind and rustling branches kept me awake. _____
4. Jane gathered up the roses and inhaled their sweet aroma. _____
5. Shivering and dripping wet, the tiny black kitten crept away. _____
6. A lawnmower's roar cut through the Sunday morning silence. _____

Circle the two things that are being compared in each sentence. Then circle whether each comparison is a simile (*S*) or a metaphor (*M*).

7. Cara's angry words felt like a slap in the face.   S   M
8. These overbaked muffins are harder than bricks.   S   M
9. In the dark of night, the snowflakes were twinkling stars. S   M
10. The twins move as slow as turtles when there's work to be done. S   M
11. Colin's new ideas are a breath of fresh air.   S   M
12. My mother is a real Martha Stewart in the kitchen.   S   M

Use sensory details to complete the word web with words and phrases that describe your school.

13.

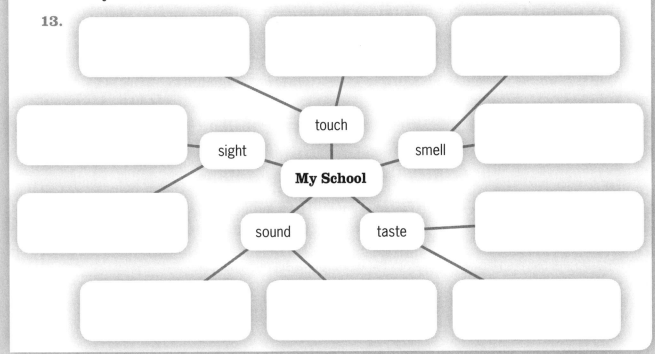

Chapter 3 • 47

Circle the word or words that correctly complete each sentence.

14. Spencer has the flu and doesn't feel (good   well) today.
15. In short races my sister runs faster (than   then) I do.
16. Please do not (set   sit) the clothes on the bed because the cat will (lie   lay) on them.
17. After I finish my homework, (may   can) I go (to   too) the park?
18. Kate will (right   write) a note on her new (stationery   stationary).

Underline the misused words in each sentence.

19. The principle past our classroom on the way to her office.
20. My friend Mary finds it hard to except complements.
21. Who's dog is lose in our front yard?
22. There new home is in the dessert, not far from the Grand Canyon.
23. Its not write to walk past you're friends and not say hello.

Circle the letter of the choice that correctly completes each sentence.

24. A dictionary thesaurus
    a. lists entry words in alphabetical order.
    b. gives synonyms for each entry word.
    c. lists guide words on the pages.
    d. does all of the above.

25. When using an indexed thesaurus, first
    a. check the table of contents.
    b. look up the word in the back section.
    c. think of a synonym for the word.
    d. do all of the above.

Use the segment from an indexed thesaurus to determine the section number of the synonym that matches how *rate* is used in each sentence.

> **rate**
> *nouns*   velocity   170.5   *verbs*   quantify   277.8
>   rank   255.7   price   630.4
>   price   644.2   deserve   601.5
>   rank   922.3

26. Most critics didn't rate this movie among the 10 best for the year. _____
27. Watch your rate of speed as you drive down the hill. _____
28. Do the players who were cut from the team rate a second chance? _____
29. What is the nightly rate for this hotel room? _____

Name _____   Date _____

CHAPTER 3 PROMPT Description

1. Read the prompt carefully.
2. Plan and organize your writing on this page.
3. Write your description on the back.
4. Revise and proofread your description.

PROMPT: Think of your favorite place to be alone. Write a description of that place for your classmates. Make certain that your writing appeals to the senses. Include a good introduction, body, and conclusion.

Plan your description here. Use a five-senses chart or a word web.

Chapter 3 • 49

Your description will be graded on how well it
- is planned.
- shows a sharp, distinct focus.
- uses illustrative content.
- is constructed in a logical order.
- is appropriate for your audience.
- uses vivid words, sensory details, and effective similes and metaphors.
- is free of grammar, usage, spelling, and punctuation errors.

Write your description here. Refer to your plan as you write. Use another sheet of paper if needed.

CHAPTER 4 TEST — Writing Skills

Write *true* or *false* for each statement about outlines.

1. An outline shows ideas in their level of importance. _____
2. Subtopics related to the main idea are labeled with numbers. _____
3. Sentences, phrases, and words can be mixed in an outline. _____
4. The periods for each type of number or letter must line up. _____

Write the items from the box to complete the outline.

> - Increases school spirit
> - Uniforms less costly than designer clothes
> - Why students should wear uniforms
> - Saves families money
> - Students' sense of belonging
> - Uniforms more durable
> - Students' greater sense of pride

5. Title: _____
   - I. _____
     - A. _____
     - B. _____
   - II. _____
     - A. _____
     - B. _____

Write three possible details for each subtopic.

6. Students should not be required to take physical education classes.
   - A. _____
   - B. _____
   - C. _____

7. Students should be required to take physical education classes.
   - A. _____
   - B. _____
   - C. _____

Use a prefix (dis-, im-, under-, mis-, non-, pre-, re-, un-, in-) and the word in parentheses to write a word that completes each sentence.

8. The store wouldn't return his deposit because it was _____. (refundable)
9. Maria grew _____ during the long wait. (patient)
10. Even though we _____, there's no reason we can't compromise. (agree)
11. Construction workers found a time capsule _____. (ground)
12. If you hurry, you may _____ the total amount you owe. (calculate)
13. Breathing is an _____ action. (voluntary)

Underline the word containing a number prefix in each sentence.

14. Ken and Jackie are the proud parents of triplets.
15. This computer's hard drive has 320 gigabytes of memory.
16. The pentathlon is one of my favorite Olympic events.
17. This children's fairy tale features an elf and a unicorn.
18. In July my great-grandmother will officially become a centenarian.
19. Which of these objects weighs about one milligram?
20. For the past decade, Mrs. Ramirez has taught math at our school.

Circle the more vivid adjective that could be used to describe each noun.

21. tree   towering   tall   big
22. trash can   encrusted   dirty   unwashed
23. car   clean   pristine   new
24. soil   waterless   dry   parched
25. ring   pretty   elaborate   nice

Circle the descriptive adjectives and prepositional phrases that modify nouns. Underline the adverbs and prepositional phrases that modify verbs.

26. The enormous elephant slowly lowered its long trunk and hungrily snatched the tiny morsel of food.
27. My multicolored kite quickly soared into the sky and flew among the fluffy white clouds.
28. The attentive crowd watched nervously as the fearsome knights on horseback in the arena reenacted a medieval joust.
29. The ecstatic teammates joyously celebrated on the baseball field while their loyal fans cheered enthusiastically from the stands.
30. A young girl with a large suitcase waited patiently for her parents.

Name _____   Date _____

CHAPTER 4 PROMPT   Persuasive Article

1. Read the prompt carefully.
2. Plan and organize your writing on this page.
3. Write your persuasive article on the back.
4. Revise and proofread your persuasive article.

> **PROMPT:** The school board is considering the cancellation of all field trips. Write a persuasive article to explain why field trips are important. Be sure to include reasons and details to support your argument.

Plan your persuasive article here. Use an idea web, an outline, or notes.

Chapter 4 • 53

Your persuasive article will be graded on how well it
- is planned.
- covers a topic that can be viewed in opposing ways.
- uses emotion and reason to convince readers to share your viewpoint.
- includes logical evidence to support your reasons.
- is organized with an introduction, a body, and a conclusion.
- includes smooth transitions between the sentences in each paragraph.
- is free of grammar, usage, spelling, capitalization, and punctuation errors.

Write your persuasive article here. Refer to your plan as you write. Use another sheet of paper if needed.

_____
_____
_____
_____
_____
_____
_____
_____
_____
_____
_____
_____
_____
_____
_____
_____
_____
_____
_____
_____
_____
_____
_____
_____

Name _____ Date _____

CHAPTER 5 TEST Writing Skills

Rewrite each sentence to correct the punctuation and capitalization as needed.

1. The reporter explained the mountain lion entered the garage through the pet door.

2. Meg said the teacher please identify the setting of the story.

3. Which of these flowers should we plant along the patio asked Trent.

Circle the letter of the quotation that makes the best introduction to an expository article titled *Perils of the Peaks*.

4. a. "At this altitude, the thin air makes it hard to breathe."—Brad Walsh
   b. "Climbing mountains is an awesome experience!"—Carl Kingston
   c. "The glistening snow-capped peaks give no hint of the dangers that await even the most experienced climbers."—Shawn Collins

Rewrite each complete quotation as a divided quotation.

5. "Your body's smallest bones and muscles are inside your ears," noted Dr. Patel.

6. "Submersibles are small submarines used to explore the ocean depths," said the scientist.

7. "When you see a red flag posted here, do not enter the water," warned the lifeguard.

Write *true* or *false* for each statement about taking notes.

8. Note-taking can only be used when listening to someone speak. _____

9. Use initials, abbreviations, and shortened words when taking notes _____

10. One way of taking notes for research is to make a KWL chart. _____

Chapter 5 • 55

Rewrite the information to show how you can use shortcuts to take notes.

11. Join us for the Community Health Fair. _____
12. It will be on Saturday, August 12th. _____
13. The fair will be held at Oak Ridge Park. _____
14. This event will last from 10:00 a.m. to 4:00 p.m. _____
15. There will be useful information, healthy foods, and games for kids. _____
16. Don't forget to enter the annual Canyon City Run for Life. _____

Circle the homophone that correctly completes each sentence.

17. Several (patience   patients) are sitting in the doctor's waiting room.
18. The diplomats found a way to restore (peace   piece) between the two countries.
19. I do not know (whether   weather) Chase will play in today's game.
20. During high (tide   tied) this part of the shore is covered in water.
21. We walked (through   threw) the garden on our way to the pool.
22. They (rode   road) their horses along the old dirt (rode   road).
23. I think (you're   your) going to regret losing (they're   their) address.
24. When I went (to   two) the mall, I bought (too   two) shirts and a jacket (two   too).

Rewrite each sentence, using the correct homophones.

25. The actors will bough to they're audience at the end of each performance.
_____

26. We took the longer, more scenic root too the beach yesterday.
_____

27. Louise, are you bringing you're sister to there party on Saturday?
_____

28. I bought sum fresh vegetables at the farmer's market two.
_____

29. Your ordering the stationary for the invitations, right?
_____

30. I tide too peaces of yellow ribbon around the tree's highest bow.
_____

Name _____ Date _____

CHAPTER 5 PROMPT — Expository Article

1. Read the prompt carefully.
2. Plan and organize your writing on this page.
3. Write your expository article on the back.
4. Revise and proofread your expository article.

PROMPT: Think of a recent school or community event that you enjoyed, such as a field trip, an assembly, a sporting event, or a celebration. Write an article for a school newspaper that reports on the event.

Plan your expository article here. Use an idea web, a KWL chart, or notes.

Your expository article will be graded on how well it
- is planned.
- has a clear focus and provides factual information.
- includes an introduction, a body, and a conclusion.
- expresses a confident voice.
- uses formal language and homophones correctly.
- gives information in different ways: quotations, statistics, and examples.
- is free of grammar, spelling, capitalization, and punctuation errors.

Write your expository article here. Refer to your plan as you write. Use another sheet of paper if needed.

_____
_____
_____
_____
_____
_____
_____
_____
_____
_____
_____
_____
_____
_____
_____
_____
_____
_____
_____
_____

Name_____ Date_____

CHAPTER 6 TEST Writing Skills

Complete the chart.

	BASE WORD	SUFFIX	NEW WORD	MEANING
1.	help	-ful	_____	_____
2.	_____	-ish	_____	like a sheep
3.	rain	-y	_____	_____
4.	cat	_____	catlike	_____
5.	_____	_____	readable	able to be read
6.	music	-al	_____	_____

Circle the word that completes each sentence. Then write the part of speech of the circled word.

7. These new shoes are quite (comfort   comfortable). _____
8. The workers complained to (management   manageable). _____
9. Call this number to (activist   activate) the account. _____
10. I (accidental   accidentally) spilled the coffee. _____
11. This parade is an annual (celebration   celebrate). _____
12. How can we (simplify   simple) this problem? _____
13. His cast was (careful   carefully) removed. _____
14. Susie's (athlete   athletic) ability is impressive. _____

Add a suffix (-able, -en, -ish, -ly, -ful, -ist, -ate, -fy, -ize) to the base word in parentheses to make a word that correctly completes each sentence.

15. The _____ made the bird disappear before our eyes. (illusion)
16. We are _____ Lisette will make a full recovery. (hope)
17. My best friend is one of the most _____ people I know. (rely)
18. I need to _____ the dog's collar so it is not so tight. (loose)
19. We _____ walked past the sleeping baby's room. (quiet)
20. Roger felt _____ in the bright red clown costume. (fool)
21. The boom of the fireworks might _____ some children. (terror)
22. Did you _____ all 50 states and their capitals? (memory)
23. Her presentation will _____ this program's positive aspects. (accent)

Chapter 6 • 59

Underline the compound part of each sentence. Write whether it is a subject (*S*), a predicate (*P*), a direct object (*DO*), or an object of a preposition (*OP*).

24. Talisa and Jamal are both English tutors. _____
25. Eddie works at the public pool in June and July. _____
26. Beth found and bought a rare book at the swap meet. _____
27. I saw Chris and Cindy at the mall today. _____
28. We are framing and displaying our favorite photos. _____
29. She added cranberries and almonds to the salad. _____
30. The graduates and their parents celebrated the day. _____
31. Our garden is full of fruits and vegetables. _____

Write *true* or *false* for each statement about writing a business letter.

32. A business letter should not include any errors. _____
33. The letter should include the recipient's professional title. _____
34. It is acceptable to use slang in a business letter. _____
35. The letter should never be more than one page long. _____
36. Include enclosures if they provide relevant information. _____
37. Write the recipient's address in the envelope's upper left-hand corner. _____
38. Do not use any abbreviations in the addresses on the envelope. _____

Use proofreading marks to correct spelling, punctuation, and capitalization errors in these addresses for an envelope.

39.

james Wiley!
1422 South Pine Avenu
SEattle, Wa 98101

                mrs Emily prescott
                Pollar Bear Parkas inc
                707 W Glacier Streeet
                Juneau ak 99801

Name_____ Date_____

CHAPTER 6 PROMPT — Business Letter

1. Read the prompt carefully.
2. Plan and organize your writing on this page.
3. Write your business letter on the back.
4. Revise and proofread your business letter.

PROMPT: Imagine you purchased a toy robot, which you now think is defective. Write a business letter to the president of Robots R Us, describing your complaint and the action you want the company to take. Make up an inside address.

Plan your business letter here. Use an idea web, an outline, or notes.

Chapter 6 • 61

Your business letter will be graded on how well it
- is planned.
- states a purpose and includes detailed information.
- uses the correct format for a business letter.
- presents ideas in a logical order.
- uses a polite, professional tone and formal language.
- is free of grammar, spelling, capitalization, and punctuation errors.
- includes a heading, an inside address, a salutation, a closing, and a signature.

Write your business letter here. Refer to your plan as you write. Use another sheet of paper if needed.

_____
_____
_____
_____
_____
_____
_____
_____
_____
_____
_____
_____
_____
_____
_____
_____
_____
_____
_____
_____

Name _____ Date _____

CHAPTER 7 TEST Writing Skills

Circle the letter of the choice that correctly completes each sentence.

1. Dialogue is
   a. a character's inner thoughts.
   b. a speech by a single character.
   c. a conversation between characters.
   d. all of the above.

2. Dialogue can be used to
   a. develop the characters.
   b. advance the plot.
   c. draw readers into the story.
   d. do all of the above.

3. Dialogue is indicated by
   a. the use of italic type.
   b. the use of quotation marks.
   c. the use of boldface type.
   d. the use of a colon.

4. Words such as *said* and *replied* are
   a. examples of metaphors.
   b. examples of personification.
   c. examples of dialogue tags.
   d. examples of homographs.

Circle the word that correctly completes each sentence.

5. "Please don't eat me!" (pleaded   bellowed) the tiny rabbit.
6. Wily Fox (sneered   wailed), "Why does this always happen to me?"
7. "Keep still," (chuckled   roared) the angry tiger, "or I will pounce on you!"
8. "Oh, wise one, how did you think of such a clever plan?" (asked   explained) Crow.
9. "I'm late! I haven't got time to wait," (whispered   snapped) the exasperated turtle.
10. "Follow me. I will lead you to a safe place," (hissed   chirped) the hungry snake.

Write a homograph from the box that matches each definition pair.

| close   pupil   firm   bluff   lean   tear |

11. a. a part of the eye   b. a student   _____
12. a. to trick   b. a cliff   _____
13. a. a drop of fluid from the eye   b. to pull apart by force   _____
14. a. nearby   b. to shut   _____
15. a. to tilt   b. thin   _____
16. a. hard   b. a company   _____

Write a homograph from the previous page that completes each sentence pair. Write *a* or *b* to show which definition is being used.

17. A _____ fell down the woman's cheek as she began to _____ up the letter.

18. The school nurse reminded the _____ to hold his head steady while she looked closely at his _____.

19. I asked the person sitting _____ to the door to _____ it for me.

20. The sales manager at this _____ has a very _____ handshake.

21. Warren tried to _____ his friend into thinking he would hang glide off the tall _____.

Write *true* or *false* for each statement about rhyming stanzas.

22. Rhyme happens when the ending syllables of words sound alike. _____

23. Meter is the number of syllables in each line of a poem. _____

24. Stanzas are made up of lines. _____

25. Each line of a poem is a complete sentence. _____

26. All poems feature an *abab* rhyme scheme. _____

Write a set of words that match each rhyme scheme.

27. abab, cdcd

_____

28. aba, bcb

_____

Complete the word web with rhyming words for *scary*.

29.

Scary

64 • Chapter 7

Name _____ Date _____

CHAPTER 7 PROMPT — Creative Writing: Trickster Tale

1. Read the prompt carefully.
2. Plan and organize your writing on this page.
3. Write your trickster tale on the back.
4. Revise and proofread your trickster tale.

PROMPT: Hummingbird wants to gather nectar from some flowers, but Hawk stands guard over her. Write a trickster tale that explains how Hummingbird is able to reach her goal.

Plan your trickster tale here. Use a story map, a time line, an idea web, or notes.

Chapter 7 • 65

Your trickster tale will be graded on how well it
- is planned.
- includes a well-developed trickster and victim.
- features a setting in the characters' natural habitat.
- includes characteristics of a trickster tale.
- uses good plot structure.
- uses literary techniques such as dialogue.
- is free of grammar, usage, spelling, and punctuation errors.

Write your trickster tale here. Refer to your plan as you write. Use another sheet of paper if needed.

_____
_____
_____
_____
_____
_____
_____
_____
_____
_____
_____
_____
_____
_____
_____
_____
_____
_____
_____
_____
_____
_____

Name_____   Date_____

CHAPTER 8 TEST   Writing Skills

Write *encyclopedia, book, periodical,* or *Web site* to identify the source of each citation.

1. Connors, Frank. Battle for the Alamo. San Antonio, TX: Cowboy Press, 2009.   _____

2. "Antarctica." World Book. 2009 ed.   _____

3. "Valley of the Kings." 25 Jan. 2010 <www.TourEgypt.com/ValleyofKings/artifacts>.   _____

4. Winters, Chris. "Creating a Compost Pile." Homegrown Gardeners 5 May 2010: 25–27.   _____

5. Sanchez, Ana. Great American Artists. New York, NY: Freedom Press, 2008.   _____

Write *true* or *false* for each statement about citing sources.

6. It is important to include a Works Cited page for all types of writing.   _____

7. Listing sources shows that your writing is reliable.   _____

8. The Works Cited page should appear at the end of the paper.   _____

9. Sources on the Works Cited page are listed in the order in which they are cited in the report.   _____

10. All the information for a book's citation can be found on the book's front cover.   _____

11. Every citation must include an author's name.   _____

12. A parenthetical notation is a short reference to a source from the Works Cited page.   _____

13. Plagiarism is rephrasing another writer's words or ideas.   _____

Underline the root in each word. Then use your understanding of the root's meaning to write the letter of the definition that matches each word.

14. audible   _____   a. a person who loves books

15. evacuate   _____   b. being or living alone

16. bibliophile _____   c. able to be heard

17. chronology   _____   d. a list of events in order of occurrence

18. solitary   _____   e. to leave an area because of an emergency

19. distort   _____   f. to twist out of shape or natural condition

Use the root in parentheses to write a word that completes each sentence.

20. Can you _____ what the movie will be about based on the trailer? (dict)
21. Martha got laser eye surgery to improve her _____. (vis)
22. I am reading a fascinating _____ about Steve Jobs. (bio)
23. The dentist must _____ my cracked tooth. (tract)
24. Jen asked the author to _____ her copy of the book. (graph)
25. A _____ studies changes in the earth's surface. (geo)

Write *encyclopedia*, *atlas*, or *almanac* to identify the best source for each example.

26. world's largest lake _____
27. short overview of animation techniques _____
28. nations on the continent of Africa _____
29. top 10 travel destinations in 2009 _____
30. history of the U.S. space program _____

Write *library*, *Internet*, or *both* to identify where you would find each item.

31. hours of operation for the Smithsonian Institution _____
32. call numbers of books about architecture _____
33. statistics for last year's baseball season _____
34. a map of Iraq that can be downloaded _____
35. source information from a book's copyright page _____

Write a word or phrase from the box to complete each sentence.

| in the library | on the Internet | catalog | almanac |
| reference | keywords | .org | .edu | atlas | fiction |

36. An encyclopedia is an example of a _____ book.
37. An _____ lists yearly statistics about a wide range of topics.
38. A library's _____ contains a list of its resources.
39. The most up-to-date information can be found _____.
40. Web sites with the extension _____ are usually reliable.
41. Use _____ to find sources of information about specific topics.

Name _____ Date _____

CHAPTER 8 PROMPT — Research Report

1. Read the prompt carefully.
2. Choose a topic and conduct research.
3. Use your notes to plan and organize your writing on this page.
4. Write your research report on the back.
5. Revise and proofread your research report.

> **PROMPT:** What Olympic sport interests you most? Do research about the history of that Olympic sport. Write a research report to show what you learned.

Use your notes to plan your research report here. Use an outline or a KWL chart.

Your research report will be graded on how well it
- is planned.
- includes a clear focus and factual information about the topic.
- is organized to include an introduction, body paragraphs, and a conclusion.
- includes parenthetical notations and a Works Cited page.
- uses formal language and a variety of sentence lengths and styles.
- uses various ways to provide information, such as quotations or examples.
- is free of grammar, usage, spelling, and punctuation errors.

Write your research report here. Refer to your plan as you write. Use another sheet of paper if needed.

___
___
___
___
___
___
___
___
___
___
___
___
___
___
___
___
___
___
___
___
___
___
___